THE TOP 10 MOST POPULAR COUNTRIES IN THE WORLD!

Geography for 3rd Grade Children's Travel Books

BABY PROFESSOR
EDUCATION KIDS

The top ten most popular countries throughout the world include FRANCE, the UNITED STATES, SPAIN, CHINA, ITALY, GERMANY, TURKEY, the UNITED KINGDOM, MEXICO, and RUSSIA. In this book, we will be learning about each country and what they have to offer.

FRANCE

Officially known as the French Republic, France is located in the western part of Europe. There are also many overseas regions and territories, but we are only discussing the territory in western Europe for this book. The territory in Europe extends from the Mediterranean Sea towards the English Channel as well as the North Sea, and from the Rhine River to the Atlantic Ocean.

RHINE RIVER

The largest city, Paris, is also its capital, which is also the main commercial and cultural center. Some of the other larger cities include Lyon, Marseille, Nice, Lille, Bordeaux, and Toulouse.

Some of the more popular sites to visit include the Eiffel Tower, the Palace of Versailles, the Louvre Museum, the Musée d'Orsay, and the Arc de Triomphe. The most popular theme park in Europe is Disneyland Paris.

RHINE RIVER

WASHINGTON D.C.

THE UNITED STATES

The United States, officially known as the United States of America, consists of 50 states, Washington D.C., five self-governing territories, as well as various possessions. Located in North America between Mexico and Canada, Washington D.C. and 48 of the 50 states are contiguous. Alaska sits in the northwest corner of North America, and is bordered to the east by Canada and Russia to the west, across the Bering Strait. Hawaii is a cluster of islands that sit in the middle of the Pacific Ocean.

The capital of the United States is Washington, D.C., which is a small city located along the Potomac River, bordering Virginia and Maryland. It is home to the three branches of government; the Capitol, the White House, as well as the Supreme Court. In addition, it is home to iconic museums and performing arts venues, including the Kennedy Center.

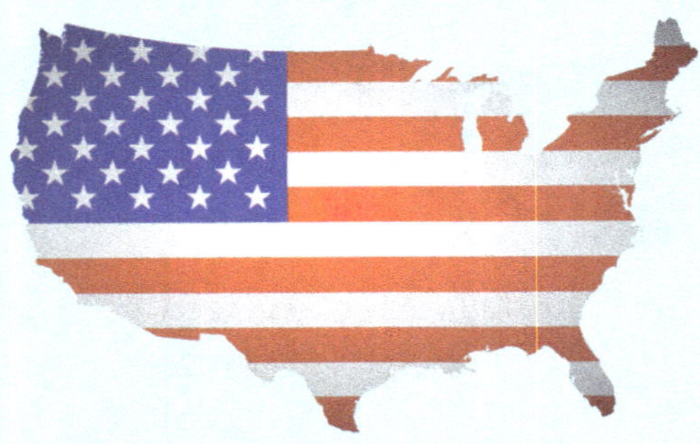

KENNEDY CENTER

In the U.S. tourism is a big industry serving millions of domestic and international tourists each year. Tourists like to visit the United States to see historical landmarks, cities, entertainment venues, and natural wonders. Americans likes to visit similar attractions, as well as vacation and recreation destinations. There is a wide range of attractions that include festivals, amusement parks, golf courses, gambling, museums, historical landmarks and buildings, galleries, and sports; to name only a few.

SPAIN

Officially known as the Kingdom of Spain, Spain is located in the southwestern area of Europe, on the Iberian Peninsula, with the Canary Islands off the North African Atlantic coast and the Balearic Islands located in the Mediterranean Sea; as well as two cities located in the mainland of North Africa and several smaller islands located near the Moroccan coast in the Alboran Sea.

BALEARIC ISLAND

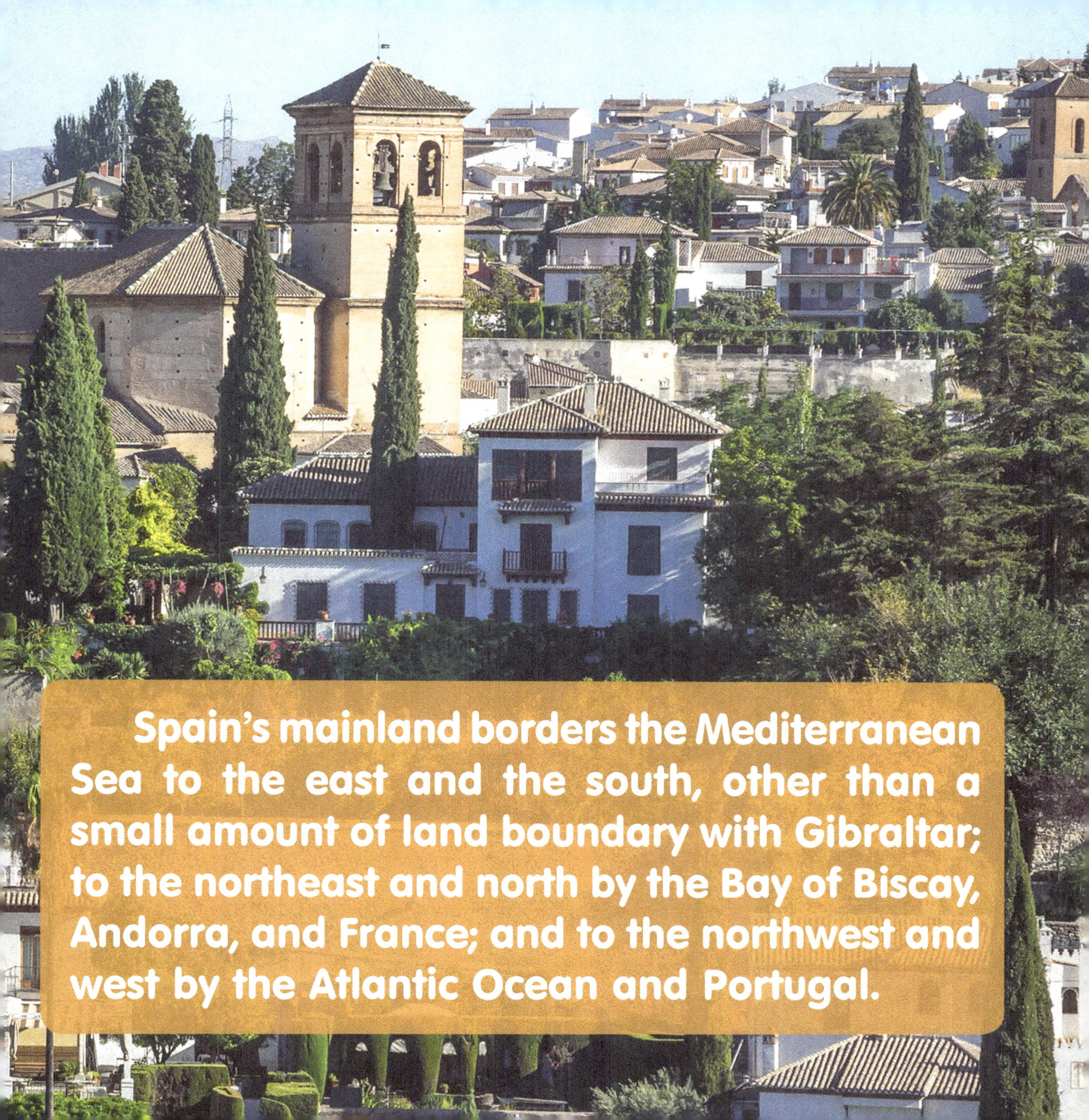

Spain's mainland borders the Mediterranean Sea to the east and the south, other than a small amount of land boundary with Gibraltar; to the northeast and north by the Bay of Biscay, Andorra, and France; and to the northwest and west by the Atlantic Ocean and Portugal.

Spain's summer resorts and beaches were the first form of tourism developed and today generates most of its income. Its extensive sandy beaches and mild climate during the entire year have been attracting tourists for decades.

CHINA

Officially known as the People's Republic of China, China is located in East Asia and is the most populous country. It covers about 3.7 million square miles and is the second-largest state by land area throughout the world.

Its long history has provided this country with several cultural relics. A symbol of this Chinese nation, the Great Wall, is one of the prime examples of its historical sites that have turned into major tourist attractions. There are over ten sections of the Wall that are open to tourists that includes blockhouses, passes, and beacon towers at Laolongtou in Hebei, Badaling in Beijing, and the Jiayuguan Pass in Gansu.

GREAT WALL OF CHINA

COLOSSEUM IN ROME

ITALY

Officially known as the Italian Republic, Italy is located in Europe at the heart of the Mediterranean Sea. It shares land borders with Switzerland, France, Slovenia, San Marino, Austria, and Vatican City. It covers an area of 116,347 square miles and the climate is mostly Mediterranean and seasonal. It is also referred to as the Boot (lo Stivale) because of its shape. Rome, the largest city in Italy, is the capital. Some of Italy's other larger cities include Milan, Naples, Turin, and Palermo.

People mainly like to visit Italy because of its rich culture, history, cuisine, art, and fashion. They also enjoy the beautiful beaches and coastline, the mountains, and the priceless ancient monuments. Some of the most-visited landmarks in Italy include the Colosseum and Roman Forum, Uffizi Gallery, Boboli Garden, Venice National Archaeological Museum, and Lake Como, to name a few.

LAKE COMO

OBERBAUM BRIDGE, BERLIN, GERMANY

GERMANY

Officially known as the Republic of Germany, Germany is located in central-western Europe. It covers an area of 137,847 square miles and its climate is mostly seasonal. Berlin is the capital and also the largest city. Some of Germany's other large cities include Hamburg, Munich, and Cologne.

Germany is known for its tourist routes, including the Wine Route, the Romantic Road, the Avenue Road, and the Castle Road. Some of its most-visited landmarks include the Cologne Cathedral, Neuschwanstein Castle, Hofbräuhaus Munich, Berlin Bundestag, and the Heidelberg Castle, to name a few. The second most popular theme park is the Europa-Park which is located near Freiburg.

TIMBURCOASTER IN EUROPA-PARK

BLUE MOSQUE ISTANBUL, TURKEY

TURKEY

Officially known as the Republic of Turkey, Turkey is located in Eurasia, but mostly in Anatolia in Western Asia, with a small area located on the Balkan Peninsula located in Southeast Europe. It borders the countries of Bulgaria and Greece to the northwest; Georgia towards the northeast; Armenia and Iran towards the east; and Syria and Iraq towards the south.

It is surrounded on three sides by different seas; the Black Sea towards the north; the Mediterranean Sea towards the south; and the Aegean Sea towards the west. Even though Istanbul is the largest city in Turkey and the main commercial and cultural center, Ankara is the capital.

PERA PALACE HOTEL

During the past 20 years, Turkey's tourism has experienced a rapid growth spurt and this makes up a big part of its economy. Some of Turkey's attractions include the Hagia Sophia, the Sultan Ahmed Mosque (the «Blue Mosque»), and the Pera Palace Hotel; to name only a few.

In addition, Istanbul has recently become one of the largest shopping areas around Europe. Turkey is home to two of the Seven Wonders of the Ancient World; the Temple of Artemis located in Ephesus, and the Mausoleum, located in Halicarnassus.

THE TEMPLE OF ARTEMIS

LONDON

THE UNITED KINGDOM

Officially known as the United Kingdom of Great Britain and Northern Ireland, the United Kingdom (UK), also known as Britain, is located in the western area of Europe. It lies off the northwestern coast of Europe's mainland and is comprised of the island of Great Britain, as well as the northeastern portion of the island of Ireland as well as several small islands. Other than its land border along the Republic of Ireland, the UK is surrounded by the Atlantic Ocean. The United Kingdom has an area of 93,600 square miles.

    Tourism is quite important to its economy. As of 2014, the United Kingdom ranked as the eighth tourist destination around the world. With 17.4 million visitors, London is the second most visited city throughout the world, following Hong Kong. Some of its top attractions include the Tower of London, Westminster Abbey, Stonehenge, as well as the Drayton Manor Theme Park; to name only a few.

STONEHENGE

METROPOLITAN CATHEDRAL IN MEXICO

MEXiCO

Officially known as the United Mexican States, Mexico is located in the southern part of North America. The United States borders it to the north; the Pacific Ocean to the west and the south; by Belize, Guatemala, and the Caribbean Sea to the southeast; and the Gulf of Mexico towards the east. It covers more than 760,000 square miles.

Mexico City is the capital of Mexico, and is also the most populous city in Mexico. Other metropolitan areas in Mexico include Guadalajara, Puebla, Monterrey, Toluca, and Tijuana.

PALACE OF FINE ARTS IN MEXICO CITY

Tourism is a huge part of Mexico's industry. Some of its attractions include colonial cities, ancient ruins, beach resorts, and cultural festivals. Its unique culture and temperate climate makes it a great place for tourists to visit. Its peak tourism seasons take place during December and mid-summer, enjoying short surges during Spring break and the week prior to Easter, when several of the resorts become a popular destination for college students traveling from the nearby United States.

RUSSIA

Officially known as the Russian Federation, Russia is located in Eurasia. It is the largest country throughout the world in land area at 6,592,800 square miles, and covers more than 1/8th of the inhabited land area of Earth. Moscow, one of the biggest cities throughout the world is the capital of Russia. Other major urban cities include Novosibirsk, Saint Petersburg, Nizhny Novgorod, Kazan, and Yekaterinburg.

KREMLIN CATHEDRAL

Russia's subtropical and warm Black Sea coast is home to several popular resorts. The Northern Caucasus mountains are home to popular ski resorts including Dombay. Lake Baikal, The Blue Eye of Siberia, is Russia's most loved natural destination.

DOMBAY IN RUSSIA

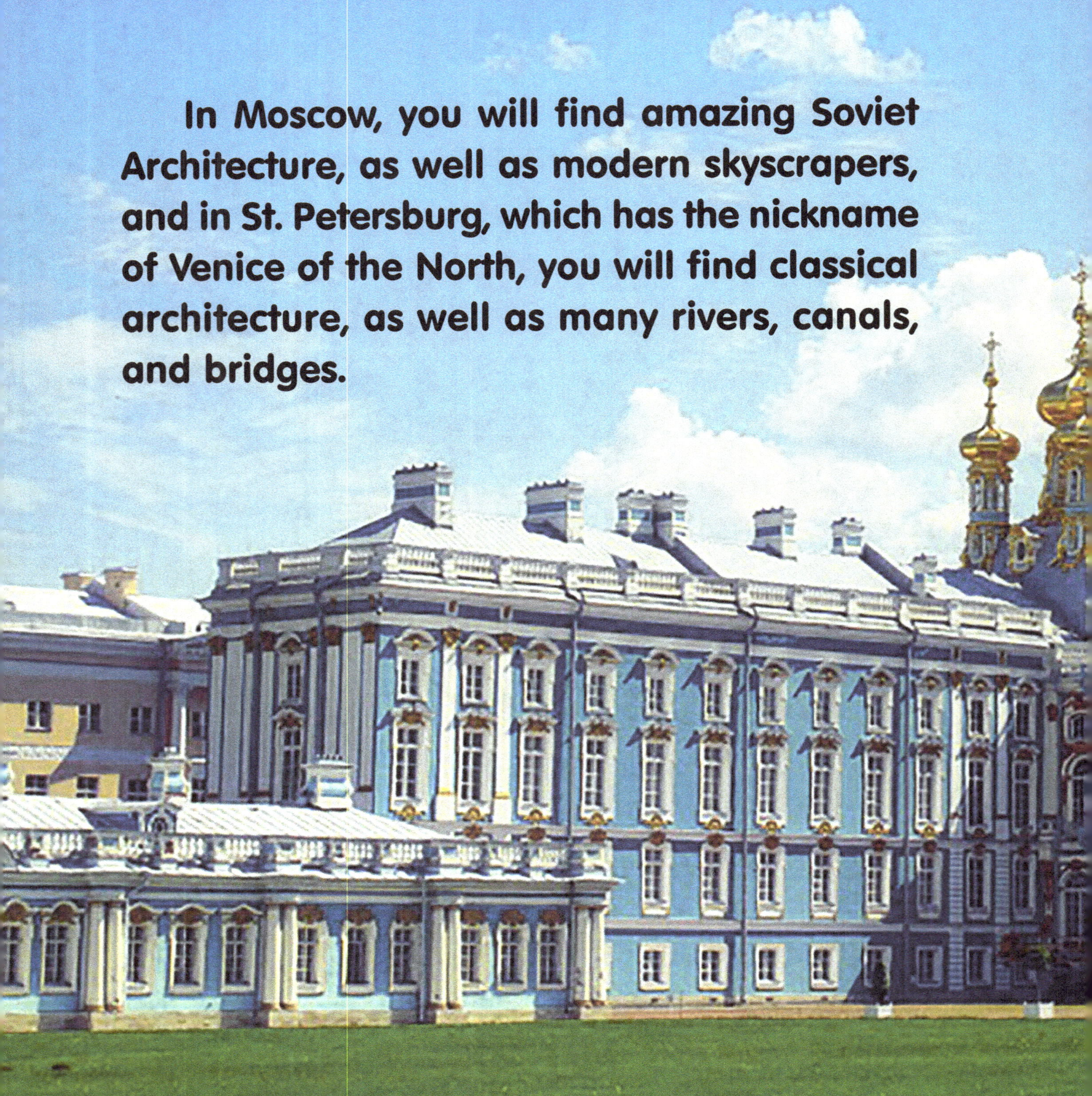
In Moscow, you will find amazing Soviet Architecture, as well as modern skyscrapers, and in St. Petersburg, which has the nickname of Venice of the North, you will find classical architecture, as well as many rivers, canals, and bridges.

ST. PETERSBURG

Each of these ten countries have so much to offer, as well as other countries that are not included in the top ten. Now that you have visited these countries in your mind, have you decided which country you would like to actually visit?

For additional information about these countries, you can visit your local library, research the internet, and ask question of your teachers, families and friends.

Visit
BABY PROFESSOR
EDUCATION KIDS
www.BabyProfessorBooks.com
to download Free Baby Professor eBooks
and view our catalog of new and exciting
Children's Books